DISCARD

Score with Sports Math

Score with Track and Field Math

Stuart A. P. Murray

Enslow Elementary
an imprint of
Enslow Publishers, Inc.
40 Industrial Road
Box 398
Berkeley Heights, NJ 07922
USA

http://www.enslow.com

Enslow Elementary, an imprint of Enslow Publishers, Inc.
Enslow Elementary® is a registered trademark of Enslow Publishers, Inc.

Copyright © 2013 by Enslow Publishers, Inc.

All rights reserved.

No part of this book may be reproduced by any means
without the written permission of the publisher.

Library of Congress Cataloging-in-Publication Data

Murray, Stuart, 1948-
  Score with track and field math / Stuart A. P. Murray.
      pages cm. — (Score with sports math)
  Audience: Grade 4 to 6.
  Summary: "Get fun track and field facts while practicing math techniques used in the sport.
Also includes math problem-solving tips"— Provided by publisher.
  Includes bibliographical references and index.
  ISBN 978-0-7660-4176-9
  1. Sports—Mathematics—Juvenile literature. I. Title.
  GV1060.55.M87 2014
  796.01'5—dc23
                                    2012039702

Future editions:
Paperback ISBN: 978-1-4644-0291-3   EPUB ISBN: 978-1-4645-1182-0
Single-User PDF ISBN: 978-1-4646-1182-7   Multi-User PDF ISBN: 978-0-7660-5811-8

Printed in China
012013 Leo Paper Group, Heshan City, Guangdong, China
10 9 8 7 6 5 4 3 2 1

To Our Readers: We have done our best to make sure all Internet Addresses in this book were active and appropriate when we went to press. However, the author and the publisher have no
control over and assume no liability for the material available on those Internet sites or on other Web sites they may link to. Any comments or suggestions can be sent by e-mail to comments@enslow.com or to the address on the back cover.

Design and Production: Rachel D. Turetsky, Lily Book Productions

Illustration Credits: AJancso/Shutterstock.com, p. 20; Andrey Yurlov/Shutterstock.com, p. 4; Aspen Photo/Shutterstock.com, pp. 18, 26, 28 (right); © 2012 Clipart.com, pp. 3, 6 (bottom), 17, 30 (bottom); Denis Kuvaev/Shutterstock.com, pp. 33, 44, 46; Diego Barbieri/Shutterstock.com, pp. 28 (left), 34 (top), 34 (bottom), 35; Herbert Kratky/Shutterstock.com, pp. 28 (top), 37; © iStockphoto.com/Nabeil Zaiton (bottom), p. 25; © iStockphoto.com/Simon A. Webber, p. 12; © iStockphoto.com/Spencer Hopkins, p. 32; © iStockphoto.com/Spencer Hopkins, p. 40 (left); © iStockphoto.com/technotr, p. 38 (left); Jamie Roach/Shutterstock.com, p. 24; Jupiterimages/Photos.com, p. 38 (bottom); Library of Congress Prints and Photographs Division, Washington, D.C., p. 8; Mark Herreid/Shutterstock.com, p. 41; Maxisport/Shutterstock.com, pp. 27, 36; Pete Niesen/Shutterstock.com, p. 6 (top); Pixland/Photos.com, p. 38 (right); Shutterstock.com, pp. 1, 5, 10, 11, 15, 20, 25 (inset), 36 (top), 39, 40 (right), 41, 42 (right), 42 (left), 43, 45 (top), 45 (bottom); Wikimedia/Erik van Leeuwen, pp. 13, 23; Wikimedia/Gio JL, p. 30 (top); Wikimedia/Ian Patterson, p. 25 (top); Wikimedia/Jonathan Bowen, p. 16; Wikimedia/*New York World-Telegram* and the *Sun* newspaper photograph collection, p. 22; Wikimedia/Tab59 (Kafuffle), p. 7; Wikimedia/Wilson Dias, Agência Brasil, p. 31.

Cover Photo: Shutterstock.com

Contents

Introduction: An Ancient Sports Tradition 4

1 Olympic Athletes 9

2 Track: Runners and Races 19

3 Field: Jumpers, Throwers, and Vaulters 29

4 The Big Meet 39

Math Problem-Solving Tips 46
Further Reading:
   Books and Web Sites 47
Index 48

Jamaican Usain Bolt won the 100m and 200m in the 2008 and 2012 Olympics.

INTRODUCTION
An Ancient Sports Tradition

The ability of early humans to run fast or to run long distances was necessary to survive. Sometimes they ran from wild animals. Sometimes they chased game, on the hunt for food.

Over the centuries humans developed axes and spears and became skilled at throwing. The most skillful athletes became leaders in hunting and war.

About three thousand years ago, the cities of ancient Greece held competitions for their best runners, throwers, and wrestlers.

The greatest events were held near Mount Olympus. There, hundreds of athletes gathered to compete in a pentathlon (five events): a foot race, long jump, javelin throw, discus throw, and wrestling. These competitions became popular around the ancient world. They developed more events in running (track), and in jumping and throwing (field).

Olympus gave its name to the greatest of all athletic competitions, the Olympic Games.

The discus throw was one of the ancient Olympic events.

Runners explode off the start line for the 100m sprint.

Modern Track and Field

Today, running, jumping, and throwing competitions are held around the world. Athletes compete in village races and on high school and college campuses. The best-known track and field competition is part of the Summer Olympics, held every four years.

The greatest athletes become famous celebrities. The whole world thrills to see them set records in speed, height, and distance. Knowing math makes track and field competitions even more exciting.

Comparing athletic records and statistics means doing math. Understanding what track and field athletes have to do to break a record or defeat an opponent involves math. In this book, you'll learn some track and field facts and you'll practice math, too.

The Summer Olympic Games

The Summer Olympics includes many sports, but track and field are still the center of attention. Track events include sprinting, middle distance and long distance races, relay races, hurdling, and fast walking. Field events include the long jump, high jump, triple jump, pole vault, shot put, javelin, discus, and hammer.

The "combined" running, jumping, and throwing events feature the ancient pentathlon as well as the heptathlon (seven events) and the decathlon (ten events). At the Olympics the world's best athletes battle for medals and international fame. They represent their countries, and their national pride makes the competition all the more intense.

Allyson Felix won the gold medal in the 2012 Olympics 200m sprint.

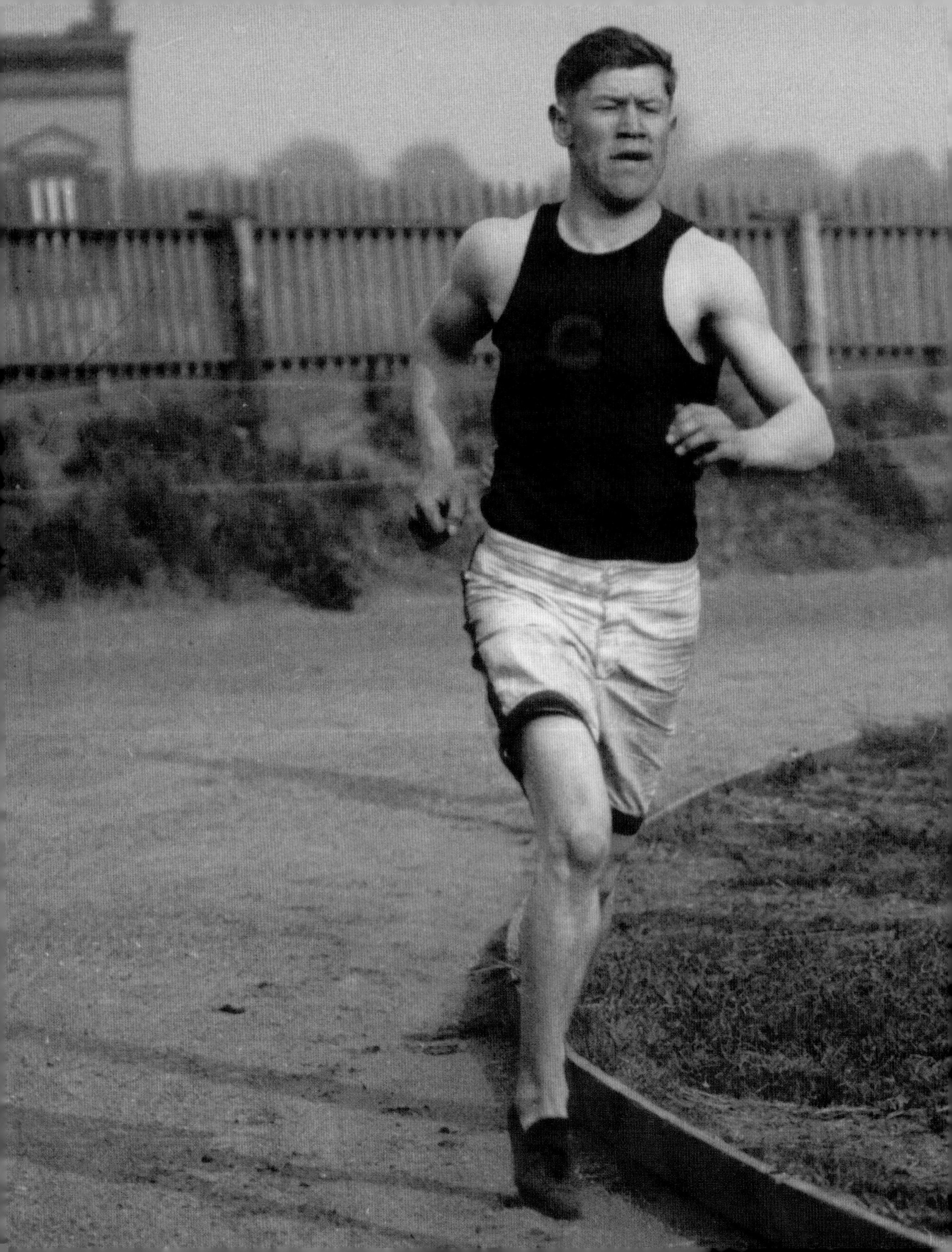

1

Olympic Athletes

Great track and field athletes push through many difficulties to be the best.

American Indian Jim Thorpe overcame poverty to win two Olympic gold medals in 1912. Englishman Roger Bannister fought disappointment and pain as he tried to run the mile in under 4 minutes. Bannister almost gave up, but in 1954 he finally succeeded. Injuries almost ended the running career of Russia's Svetlana Masterkova, but she came back to set the women's record in the mile.

The hard work for track and field excellence continues today.

Jim Thorpe trains on a track in the early 1900s.

Many national flags fly at the Olympics.

The modern Olympics

The 2012 Summer Olympic Games in London had 10,820 athletes from 204 countries. There were 302 events in 26 sports, from archery to wrestling. Track and field had 47 events, with 2,000 athletes from 201 nations.

Q: Look at the number of countries in the Olympics and the number of countries that took part in track and field. Write a fraction to show how many of the countries had track and field teams.

A: 201 countries out of 204 total teams at the Olympics had track and field teams.
201 is a fractional part of the total, 204.
Make 201 the numerator and 204 the denominator.
The fraction $201/204$ shows that almost every country had a track and field team.

Olympic medal winners

Athletes receive a gold medal for first place, silver for second, and bronze for third. In the 2012 Olympics, the United States men's and women's track and field teams won 9 gold, 13 silver, and 7 bronze medals.

Q: How many total medals did the United States track and field teams win?

A: Add: 9 + 13 + 7 = 29 medals

The United States, Russia, and Jamaica were the top medal winners. Russia won 8 gold, 5 silver, 5 bronze. Jamaica won 4 gold, 4 silver, 4 bronze.

Q: Which country won the most track and field medals? Which was second? third?

A: The United States had 29. Add up Russia's medals and then add up Jamaica's medals and compare the three totals.
Russia: 8 + 5 + 5 = 18
Jamaica: 4 + 4 + 4 = 12
The United States had the most: 29. Russia was second and Jamaica was third.

The world's top athlete

The Olympics decathlon winner is said to be the greatest athlete in the world. *Decathlon* means "ten events." These include sprinting, distance running, jumping, and throwing. The decathlete who earns the most points wins the decathlon. In the 2012 Olympics, American Ashton Eaton won the gold in the men's decathlon.

Q: Eaton had 8,869 total points. Fellow American Trey Hardee was second, with 8,671. How many more points did Eaton earn than Hardee?

A: Subtract Hardee's 8,671 from Eaton's 8,869.
8,869 − 8,671 = 198 more points

Eaton was first in 3 of the 10 decathlon events, second in 2 others, and third in one event. A hundred years earlier, in 1912, American Jim Thorpe won the Olympics decathlon: first in 4 events and third in 4 others.

Q: Who had the most "places" (1st, 2nd, 3rd), Eaton or Thorpe?

A: Add each decathlete's places and compare the totals.

Eaton: 3 (1st) + 2 (2nd) + 1 (3rd):

3 + 2 + 1 = 6 places

Thorpe: 4 (1st) + 4 (3rd)

4 + 4 = 8 places

Ashton Eaton was the 2012 Olympics men's decathlon champion.

Beating the favorite

The favorite to win the 1912 Olympic decathlon was Sweden's Hugo Wieslander. Jim Thorpe came from a poor Oklahoma family and was not known as a track star. He faced 29 top decathletes from 12 nations.

The 1912 Olympic decathlon

100-meter dash			Discus throw		
Thorpe	3rd	904 pts	Thorpe	3rd	829 pts
Wieslander	13th	762 pts	Wieslander	4th	803 pts

Long jump			110-meter hurdles		
Thorpe	3rd	830 pts	Thorpe	1st	943 pts
Wieslander	8th	740 pts	Wieslander	11th	791 pts

Shot put			Pole vault		
Thorpe	1st	809 pts	Thorpe	3rd	751 pts
Wieslander	4th	734 pts	Wieslander	8th	670 pts

High jump			Javelin		
Thorpe	1st	958 pts	Thorpe	4th	748 pts
Wieslander	4th	790 pts	Wieslander	1st	878 pts

400-meter dash			1500-meter run		
Thorpe	4th	857 pts	Thorpe	1st	779 pts
Wieslander	8th	804 pts	Wieslander	6th	750 pts

Q: Look at the chart. Note where Thorpe placed in each event. What do you see about how he did in all the events?

A: He finished 4th or better every time. He also beat Wieslander in all but the javelin.

Thorpe won the decathlon with a total of 8,408 points to Wieslander's 7,722 points.

Q: How many more points did Thorpe have than Wieslander?

A: Subtract 7,722 from 8,408:

8,408 − 7,722 = 686 more points for Thorpe

Q: Which event gave Thorpe the most points?

A: The high jump: 958

Q: Which event gave Wieslander the fewest points?

A: The pole vault: 670

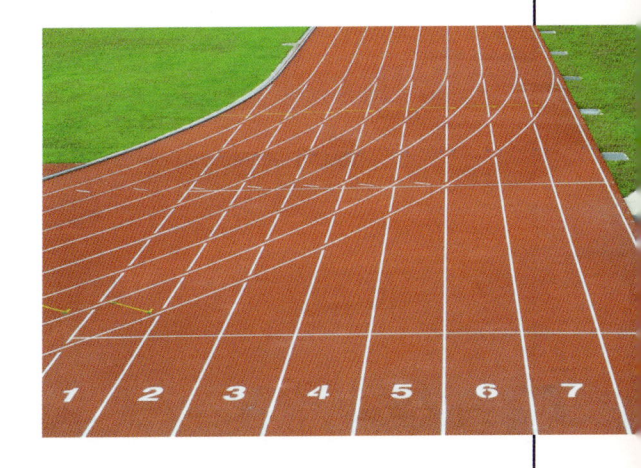

The mile

Official world track and field records were first kept in 1912. Soon, many runners were trying hard to run the mile under 4 minutes. In 1954, English student Roger Bannister finally broke the 4-minute mile.

Q: In track, times are measured in minutes, seconds, and tenths or hundredths of a second. Bannister's time was 3:59.4. How do you express this time in words?

A: Three minutes, fifty-nine and four tenths seconds. Or, three fifty-nine point four.

Q: How many years after 1912 did Bannister run the mile under 4 minutes?

A: Subtract 1912 from 1954: 1954 − 1912 = 42 years

A plaque marks the first sub 4-minute mile.

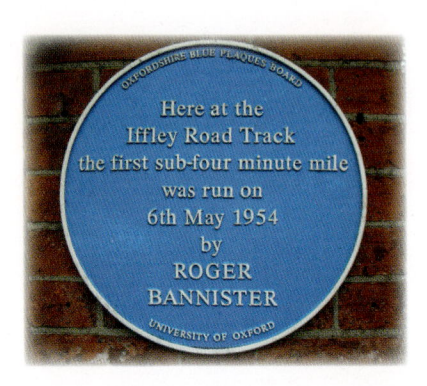

Many runners have beaten Bannister's mile record. In 1999 Hicham El Guerruj of Morocco set the current record. He ran the mile in 3:43.13.

Q: How many seconds faster was El Guerruj than Bannister? Round their times to the nearest second.

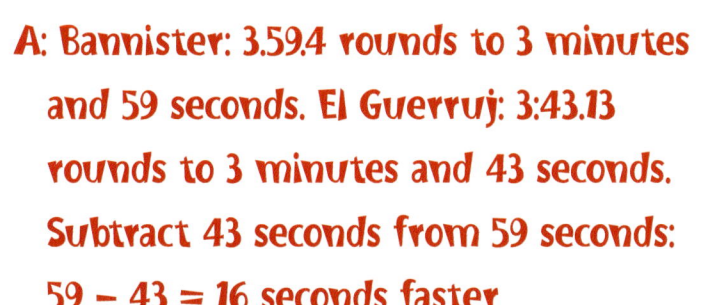

A: Bannister: 3:59.4 rounds to 3 minutes and 59 seconds. El Guerruj: 3:43.13 rounds to 3 minutes and 43 seconds. Subtract 43 seconds from 59 seconds:
59 − 43 = 16 seconds faster

In 1996 Russia's Svetlana Masterkova set the women's world record for the mile: 4:12.56.

Q: Express Masterkova's time in words.
A: Four minutes, twelve and fifty-six hundredths seconds.

Q: A yard is three feet. The mile is 5,280 feet. How many yards are in a mile?
A: Divide 5,280 by 3:
5,280 ÷ 3 = 1,760 yards

USA
WOTE
ETH
PENN RELAYS
USA
the WORLD
MANZANO
USA
PENN RELAYS

2

Track: Runners and Races

The sprints can be the most exciting foot races of all. A fast start and lightning speed are needed to win. But middle distance and long distance races call for strength and the ability to run hard for several long minutes.

Then there are the hurdles, with runners leaping over barriers while sprinting. Relay races require a team of four athletes to take turns sprinting around the track.

Many track meets are held in every country, but world records are set only in official competitions. The Summer Olympics is the most famous meet and often produces world record holders.

An American relay runner has an opponent close behind.

Distance running

Middle distance events include the 800 meters, 1500 meters, 1600 meters, and the mile (5,280 feet). Americans do not use meters for measuring, except in track and field. All international races are in meters (m), except for the mile.

Q: One meter equals about 39 inches; 1 yard is 36 inches. How much longer in inches is a meter than a yard?

A: Subtract 36 inches from 39 inches:
39 − 36 = 3 inches longer

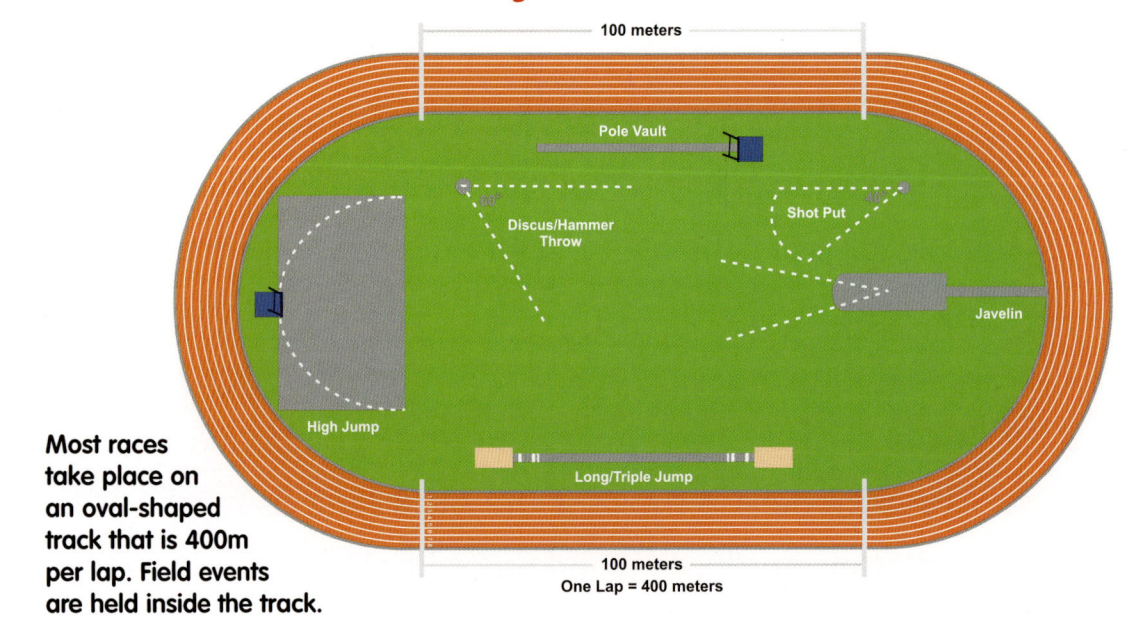

Most races take place on an oval-shaped track that is 400m per lap. Field events are held inside the track.

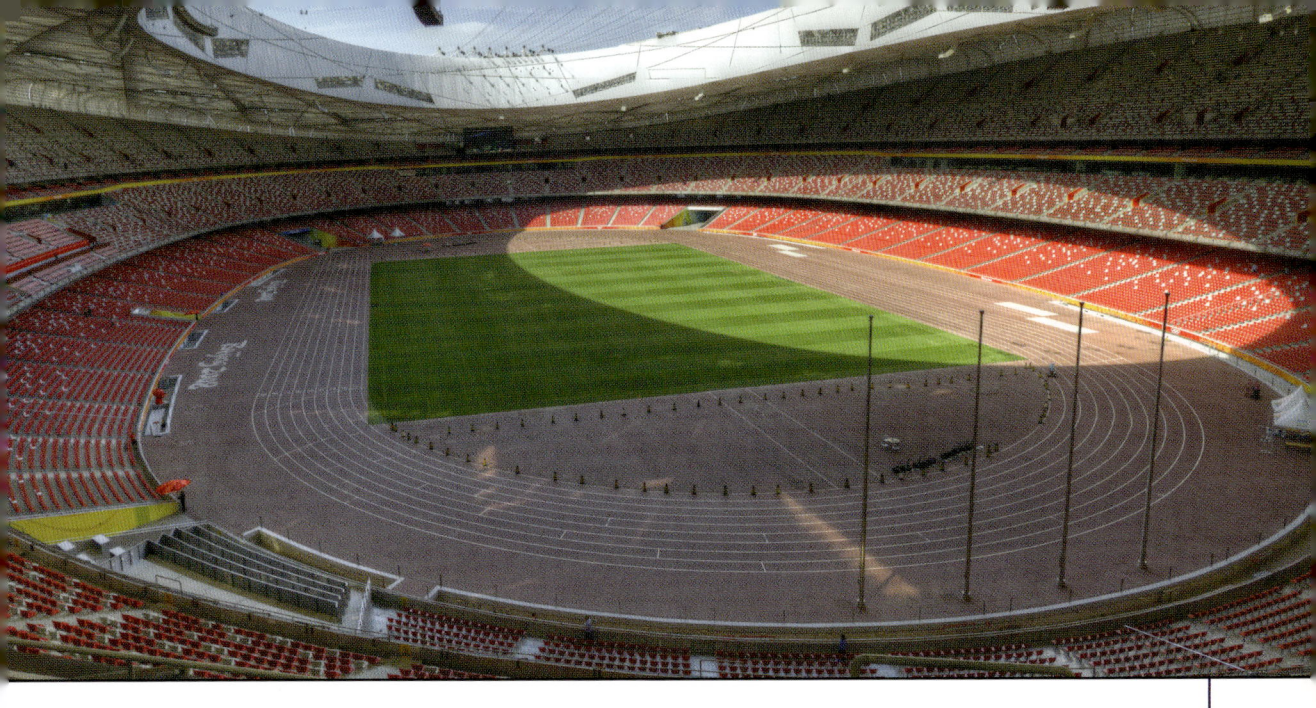

Bird's Nest Stadium in Beijing, China.

Q: How many times do runners go around a 400m track in a race of 1,600m?

A: Divide 1,600 by 400:
1,600 ÷ 400 = 4 times

Q: One lap of the track of the stadium at Olympus in ancient Greece was 212m. How much shorter was that track than the modern track?

A: Subtract 212 from 400:
400 − 212 = 188
The Olympus track was 188m shorter than the modern track.

Wilma Rudolph was called the "fastest woman on earth" in the 1960s.

Wilma Rudolph

Rudolph was ill as a child and wore a leg brace. When she was older, she began running. In 1960, she was the first woman to win three Olympic gold medals: the 100m, the 200m, and the 400m relay (with three teammates).

The world's speediest

Jamaica's Usain Bolt holds the men's records for the 100m and 200m, and American Florence Griffith-Joyner has both women's records. South Africa's Oscar Pistorius holds the Paralympics 400m record.

Q: In 1960 American Wilma Rudolph's 200m time of 23.2 seconds set a women's world record. Look at the chart to see Griffith-Joyner's 200m time. How much faster was Griffith-Joyner?

A: Subtract Griffith-Joyner's 21.3 from Rudolph's 23.2:
23.2 − 21.3 = 1.9 seconds
Griffith-Joyner was 1.9 seconds faster.

Q: What was the average time to run 400 meters for Johnson, Koch, and Pistorius? First round their times to the nearest second.

A: 43.9 rounds to 44, 47.6 rounds to 48; Pistorius is 45.
Add their times:
44 + 48 + 45 = 137
Divide by 3:
137 ÷ 3 = 45.7

World Records

100m dash	Time in seconds
Usain Bolt	9.6
Florence Griffith-Joyner	10.5
200m dash	
Usain Bolt	19.2
Florence Griffith-Joyner	21.3
400m dash	
Michael Johnson	43.9
Marita Koch	47.6
Paralympics 400m dash	
Oscar Pistorius	45.0

Oscar Pistorius lost his lower legs as a child. The Paralympics are for athletes with disabilities.

The hurdles

There are 100m hurdles for women and 110m hurdles for men. Both men and women run 400m hurdles. The runner sprints full speed while jumping over ten hurdles on the way to the finish line. Any mistake can cause the runner to fall when going over a hurdle.

A hurdler shows perfect form in clearing the hurdles.

Q: In the 400m hurdles, the ten hurdles are spaced 35m apart. How many meters of the 400m are between the first and last hurdles?

A: Draw a diagram showing the ten hurdles and count the spaces between hurdles: 9 spaces. Multiply 9 times the 35m between hurdles: 9 × 35 = 315m of space between the first and last hurdles

The 400m hurdles is one of the toughest sports events of all.

Q: The run up to the first hurdle is 45m. How many meters is it from the last hurdle to the finish line?

A: Add 45m to the 315m of hurdles:

45 + 315 = 360m

Subtract 360 from the event distance of 400m:

400 − 360 = 40m for the final sprint

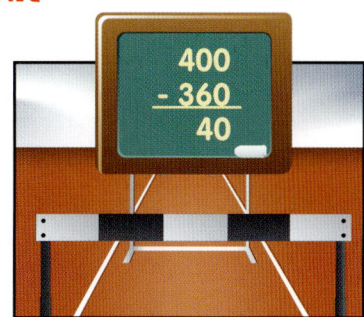

Relay athletes hand off a baton (stick) to the next teammate while both are running.

Teamwork and speed

The first runners of a relay team have to work hard so that their fourth teammate has a chance to win the final sprint. In 1960, Wilma Rudolph's four-woman relay team set a 400m world record (44.5 seconds).

Q: What was the relay team's average time for 100 meters?

A: Find the number of 100m in 400m by dividing 400 by 100:

$400 \div 100 = 4$

There are four 100m in the 400m dash.

Find the average time per 100m by dividing the seconds by 4:

$44.5 \div 4 = 11.1$

11.1 seconds was the relay team's average time per 100m.

Q: Follow the same steps and find the average time per 100m for Rudolph's 200m dash (23.2 seconds) in 1960.

A: Divide 200 by 100:

200 ÷ 100 = 2

Divide 23.2 seconds by 2:

23.2 ÷ 2 = 11.6

11.6 seconds was Rudolph's average time.

Q: Which average time for 100m was the fastest?

A: Subtract the smaller average time (11.1) from the larger (11.6):

11.6 − 11.1 = .5 seconds

The relay team averaged half a second faster per 100m.

Runners sprint away after the baton handoff in a 400m relay.

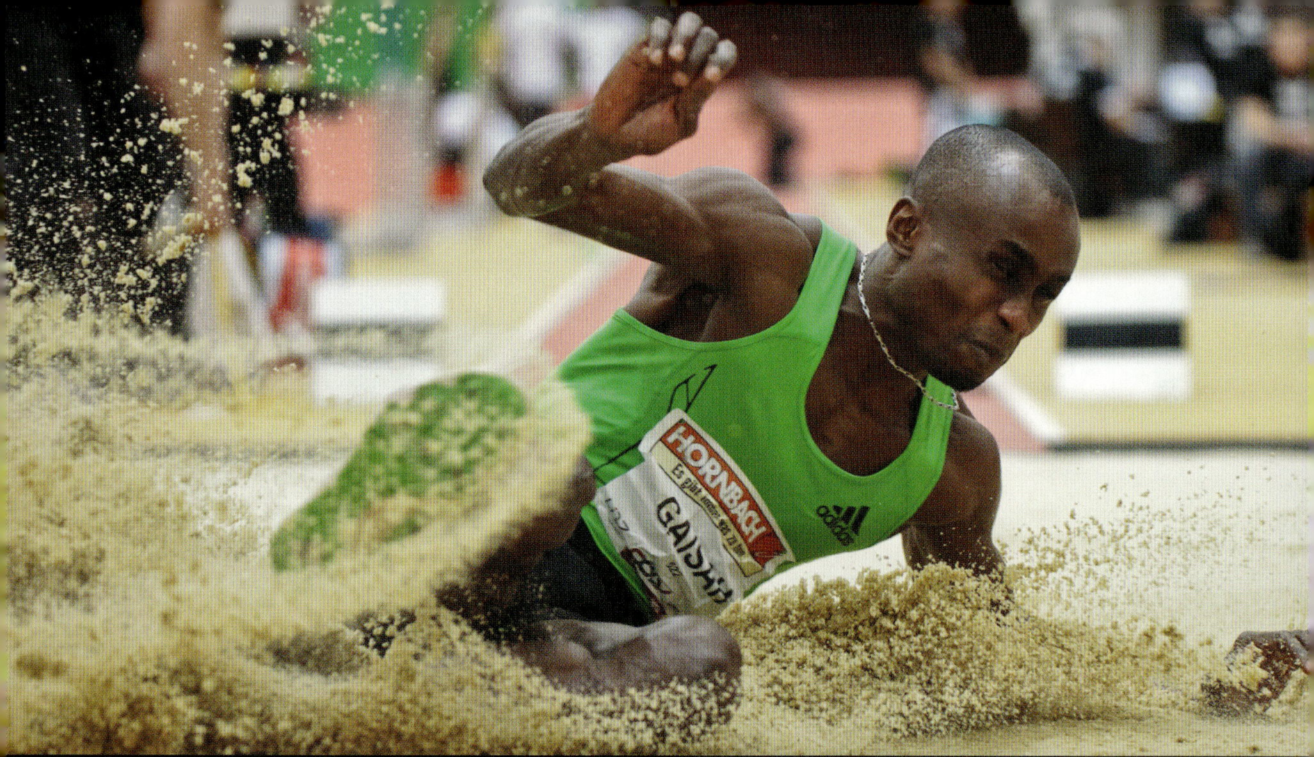
HORNBACH
adidas

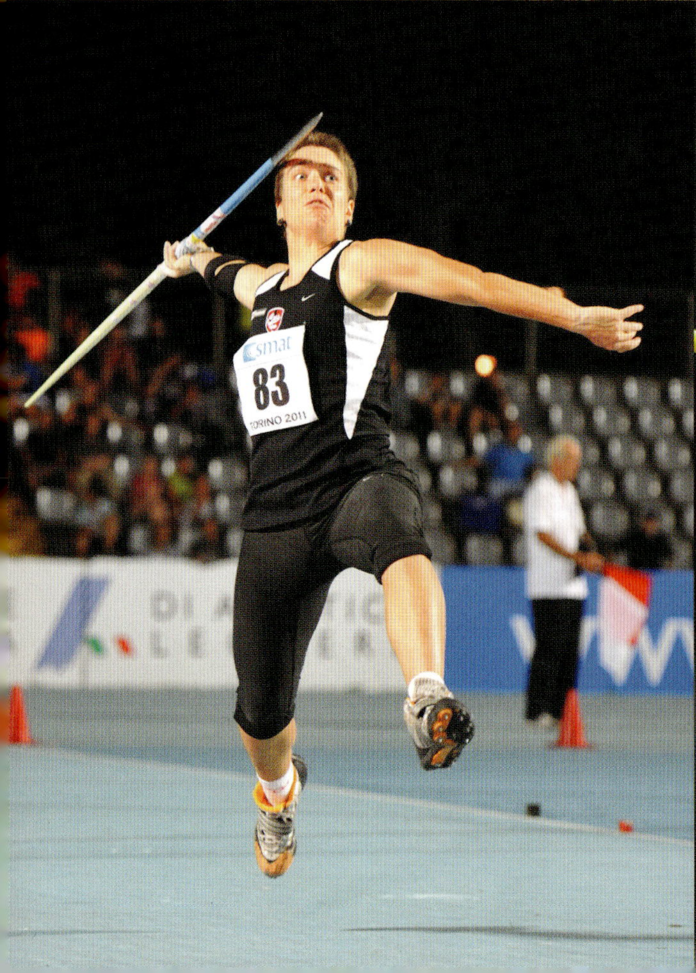
smat
83
TORINO 2011

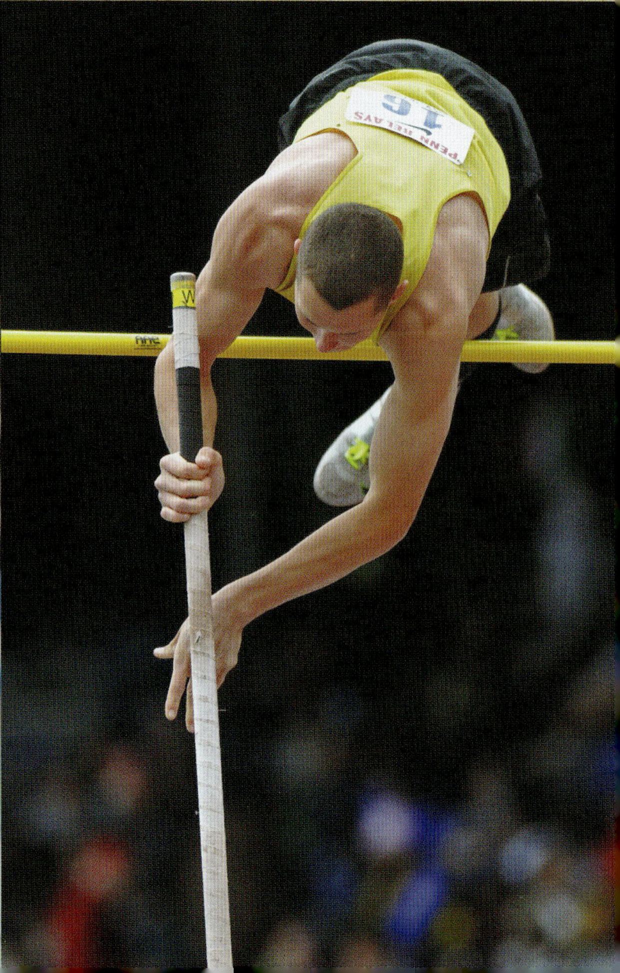
PENN RELAYS
16

3

Field: Jumpers, Throwers, and Vaulters

Jumping and throwing are the competitions in field events. Who can jump longer or higher has always been a favorite competition for young people.

In the days when there were few bridges, travelers used poles to "vault" across streams. Today, pole-vaulters compete to see who can go the highest.

Ancient athletes took pride in throwing the discus well. Javelin throwing was also important because it was how soldiers trained to use spears.

The shot put came from throwing cannonballs (shot) for fun in military camps.

Athletes compete in the long jump, javelin throw, and pole vault.

Pole vault

Pole-vaulters and high jumpers try to get over a bar without knocking it off. If they fail, they are out of the competition. The bar is raised a little higher until only one athlete remains: the winner.

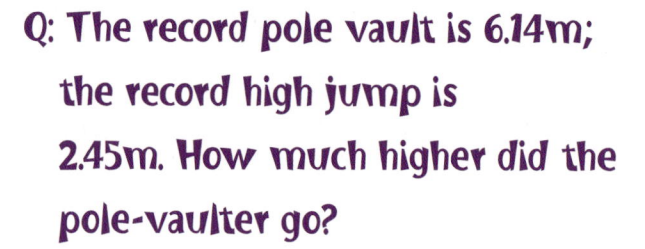

A pole-vaulter uses a pole to help him over the bar.

Q: The record pole vault is 6.14m; the record high jump is 2.45m. How much higher did the pole-vaulter go?

A: Subtract 2.45m from 6.14m:

6.14 − 2.45 = 3.69m higher

Ukrainian Sergey Bubka set the outdoor pole-vaulting record of 6.14m in 1994. Yelena Isinbayeva, a Russian, set the women's record, 5.06m, in 2009.

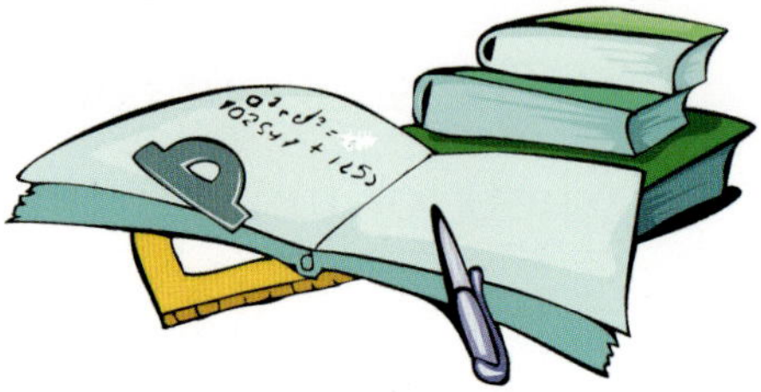

Q: Isinbayeva is 1.74m tall. How many times would her height fit into her record pole vault?

A: Divide 1.74 into 5.06:

5.06 ÷ 1.74 = 2.91

Almost three times.

Q: How much higher would Isinbayeva have to go to tie Bubka?

A: Subtract her 5.06m from his 6.14m:

6.14 − 5.06 = 1.08m

She needs another 1.08m.

Yelena Isinbayeva is the world's best female pole-vaulter.

High jump

High jumpers have to spring over the bar without using anything to help them. To win, they have to leap higher than they are tall.

Q: The ends of a high jump bar rest on posts at exactly the same height from the ground. Is the bar perpendicular, parallel, or intersecting with the ground?

A: Draw a diagram of the ground, posts and bar. The bar is parallel with the ground.

Cuba's Javier Sotomayor has the world high jump record, 2.45m. Sotomayor won Olympic gold in 1992. He missed the 1996 Olympics because he was injured. He won silver in 2000, his last Olympics. Cuba did not enter the two Olympics at the start of his career.

Q: Sotomayer's silver medal jump was 2.32m. How much higher was his record jump?

A: Subtract 2.32m from 2.45m:
   2.45m − 2.32m = 0.13m

The women's high jump record, 2.09m, was set in 1987 by Bulgaria's Stefka Kostadinova.

Q: Kostadinova is 1.80m tall. How much higher than her head did she jump to set the record?

A: Subtract her height, 1.80m, from 2.09m:

2.09 − 1.80 = .29m

She jumped .29m (11 3/8 in.) higher than her head.

Most high jumpers use the "flop" method to clear the bar.

Hopping, stepping, and jumping

Long jumpers run then leap from a marker into a sandpit. Triple jumpers sprint, hop from the marker, step, and then jump into the sandpit. Jumps are measured to the sand print nearest the marker.

Q: As a long jumper lands he falls backward to sit on the sand. His footprints are 7.5m from the marker. His seat's print in the sand is 7.1m from the marker. What is the distance of his jump?

A: The jump is measured to the print closest to the marker: his seat, 7.1m.

The long jumper (above) flies feet first. The triple jumper (left) runs and then hops, steps, and jumps.

A triple jumper falls sideways on landing.

Q: How much did the jumper lose?

A: Subtract 7.1m from 7.5m:

7.5 − 7.1 = .4

The jumper lost .4m (15 in.)

Q: A triple jumper's total distance was 10.9m. Her hop was 2.7m and her step was 4.1m. How long was her jump?

A: Add her hop and step:

2.7 and 4.1 = 6.8

Subtract 6.8 from the total distance, 10.9:

10.9 − 6.8 = 4.1m, the length of the jump

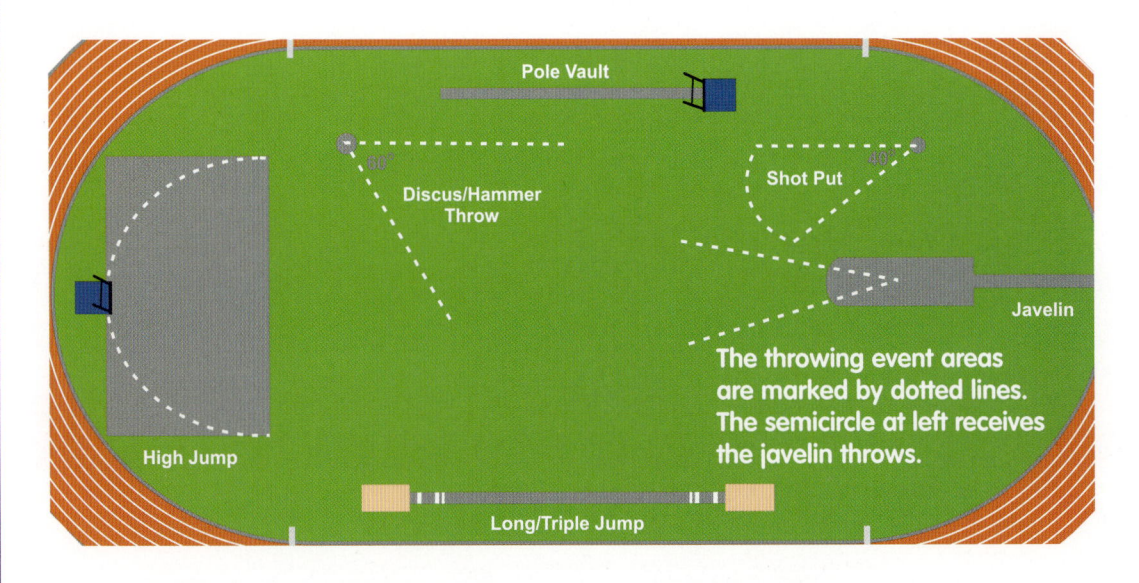

Pole Vault
Discus/Hammer Throw
Shot Put
Javelin
High Jump
Long/Triple Jump

The throwing event areas are marked by dotted lines. The semicircle at left receives the javelin throws.

Throwing for distance and power

The javelin, discus, and shot put are the best-known throwing events. The javelin is a spear. The discus is circular and zooms through the air like a flying saucer. The shot is a 16-pound metal ball that is "put," with a push, rather than a throw.

A javelin begins its flight.

Q: In the diagram above look at the three areas for these events. What kind of angles do they form?

A: They are all acute angles (less than 90°).

Q: Which throwing event needs the most room for the thrower?
A: The javelin.

Q: Which event needs the least room?
A: The shot put.

The javelin world record is 98.5m. The shot put record is 23.1m. The discus record is 74.0m.

Q: Round the records for the discus, shot, and javelin to the nearest meter.
A: Javelin: 99m. Shot: 23m. Discus: 74m.

Q: Place these distances in order, from lowest to highest.
A: 23m, 74m, 99m

discus

The discus is a real flying saucer. This one is in the upper right of the picture.

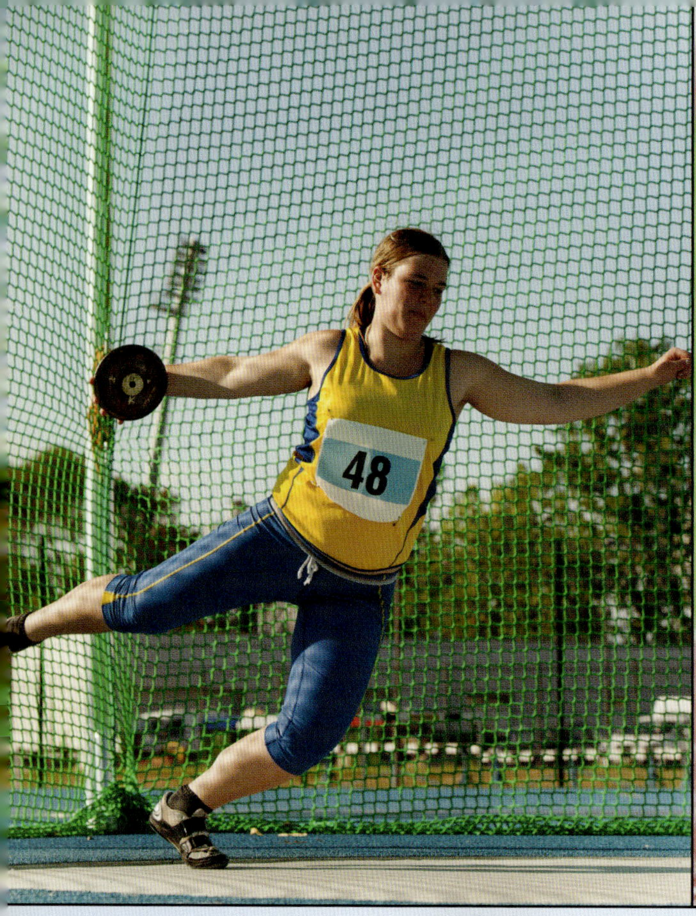
48

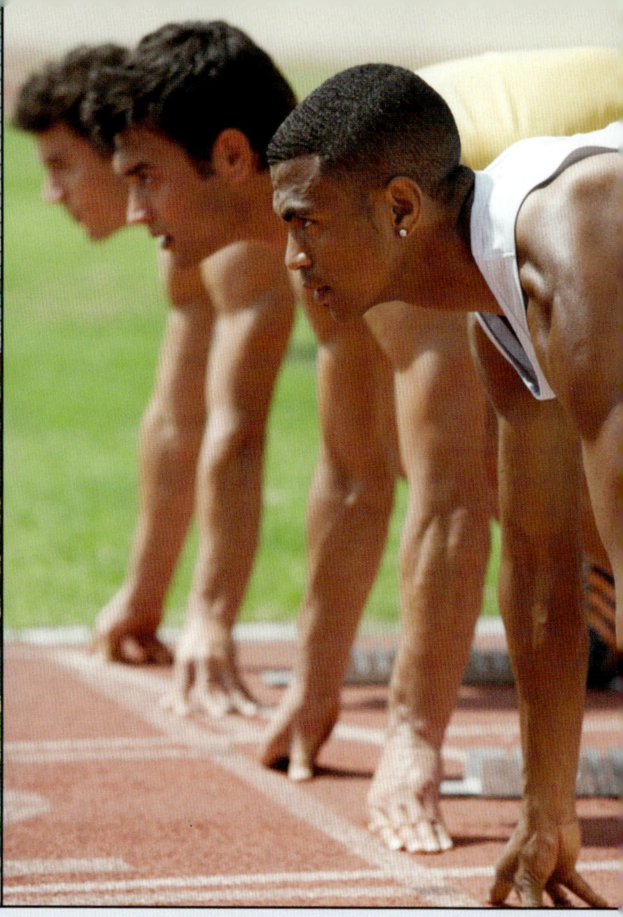

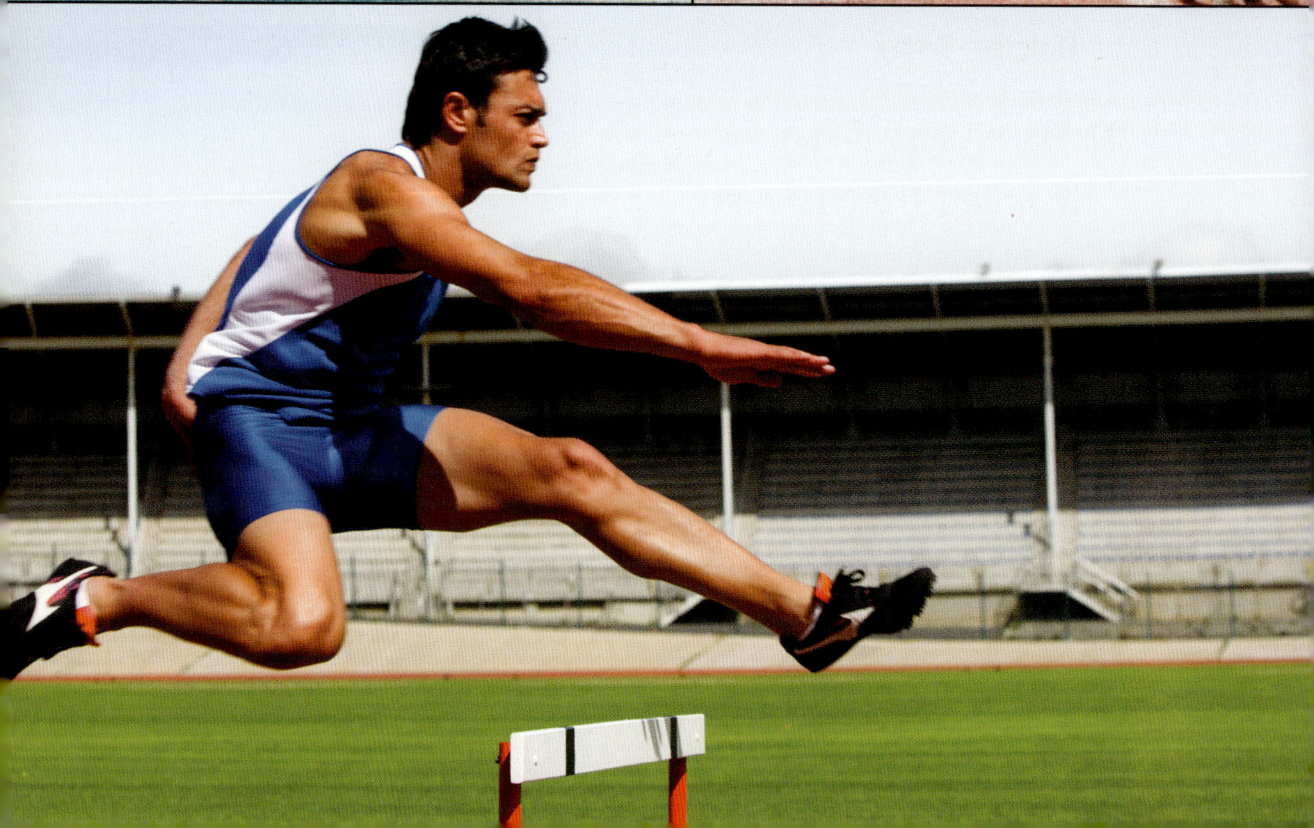

4

The Big Meet

Track and field competitions are called "meets." The meet between Ross Corners and Highfield is always exciting. Both high schools have top track and field teams. Highfield has one of the best triple jumpers in the state. Ross Corners has very good sprinters, especially on its 400m relay team.

In this meet, athletes get 5 points for first place, 3 for second, and 1 for third. In relay races, only first place gets points (5). To get enough points to win, teams need as many places as possible. Of course, everyone wants to win.

A discus thrower spins, sprinters get set, and a hurdler clears the hurdle.

Ross Corners vs. Highfield

In track meets the teams win some events and come in second or third in others. In the end the team with the most total points from all the events wins the meet.

Q: This meet has 8 running events, 6 field events, and one relay race. How many events are there?

A: Add the types of events together:
8 + 6 + 1 = 15 events

Q: How many points are there to be won?

A: The relay has 5 points and the other 14 events have 9 points each: 5 for first, 3 for second, 1 for third.

Multiply 9 points by 14 events:
9 × 14 = 126 points
Add 5 points for the relay:
126 + 5 = 131 total points

The pole bends and gives spring to the pole-vaulter.

Highfield takes first and second in both the pole vault and the shot put. Ross Corners gets first and second in the 100m dash and the 400m dash. Both teams have 2 firsts, 2 seconds, and also 2 thirds.

Q: What is the meet score?
A: Add the points together and compare them:
   For 1sts: 2 × 5 = 10 points
   For 2nds: 2 × 3 = 6 points
   For 3rds: 2 × 1 = 2
   Add the total points:
   10 + 6 + 2 = 18 points each

A shot putter is about to put the shot.

Down to the last

The meet stays very close. It has only two events to go: the triple jump and the 400m relay. Highfield has 6 firsts, 7 seconds, and 10 thirds. Ross Corners has 7 firsts, 6 seconds, and 3 thirds.

Q: How many points does each team have?
**A: Multiply the places by their point values.
Then add the products together.**

Highfield		Ross Corners	
6 firsts:	6 × 5 = 30	7 firsts:	7 × 5 = 35
7 seconds:	7 × 3 = 21	6 seconds:	6 × 3 = 18
10 thirds:	10 × 1 = 10	3 thirds:	3 × 1 = 3
	Total: 61		Total: 56

So, the meet score is Highfield 61 and Ross Corners 56. The triple jump has 9 possible points; the relay has 5. (Remember, first place in the relay gets all 5 points.)

Q: How many points are there still left to get?

A: Add 9 for the triple jump to 5 for the relay race: 9 + 5 = 14 points left

The triple jump is Highfield's best event. They usually win all 9 points. Even if Ross Corners wins the 400m relay and takes the 5 points, they might lose.

A relay runner waits for the baton handoff.

The triple jumper's "step" is always a big one.

A personal best, and worst

Before the triple jump, the starting gun goes off for the 400m relay. Everyone is cheering for their own team, and Ross Corners pulls ahead. Ross Corners wins and gets 5 points.

Q: Now what is the meet score?
A: Add 5 to Ross Corners' 56:
   5 + 56 = 61
   The meet is tied 61–61.

The first Highfield triple jumper gets 12.9m. Then, to everyone's surprise, the Ross Corners jumper gets his best ever: 13.5m. It is .5m longer than his best jump before this meet.

Q: How long was his other jump?

A: Subtract .5 from 13.5:

13.5 − .5 = 13m was his earlier best jump.

The top Highfield triple jumper now goes. But he fouls by going past the marker. He has two more chances. His next jump is 13.3m. Then, his last jump looks great, but he falls backward and sits down in the sand at 12.7m.

Q: Who got first, second, and third?

A: Put the three best distances in order, first to third:
1st − Ross Corners: 13.5m
2nd − Highfield: 13.3m
3rd − Highfield: 12.9m

Q: Now what is the meet score?

A: Ross Corners got 5 for first.
Highfield got 3 for second + 1 for third = 4 points.
Ross Corners: 61 + 5 = 66 points
Highfield: 61 + 4 = 65 points

Ross Corners wins 66–65!

Math Problem-Solving Tips

✏️ Always read the problem completely before beginning to work on it.

✏️ Make sure you understand the question.

✏️ Some problems take more than one step to find the final answer.

✏️ Don't think you always have to use every number in the problem. Some numbers are extra information that are not needed for the calculations.

✏️ If you know your answer is wrong but can't find the mistake, then start again on a clean sheet of paper.

✏️ Don't get upset! You can solve problems better when you're calm.

✏️ If you're stuck on a problem, skip it and go on with the rest of them. You can come back to it.

Further Reading

Books

The Complete Book of Math, Grades 3 and 4. Greensboro, N.C.: American Education Publishing, 2009

Connolly, Sean. *The Book of Perfectly Perilous Math.* New York: Workman Publishing Company, 2012.

Fitzgerald, Theresa. *Math Dictionary for Kids.* Waco, Tex.: Prufrock Press, Inc., 2011.

Web Sites

Drexel University. The Math Forum @ Drexel University
<http://www.mathforum.org/k12/mathtips>
K–12 math problems, puzzles, and tips and tricks. The Math Forum of Drexel University is a leading online resource for improving math learning, teaching, and communication.

IXL Learning © 2012 IXL Learning.
<http://www.ixl.com>
Math practice of all kinds, through interactive games and practice that make math practice fun.

Index

A
acute angle, 36
addition, 11, 13, 15, 25, 35, 40–44
American, 9, 12, 18, 20, 22–23
archery, 10
average, 23, 26–27

B
Bannister, Roger, 9, 16–17
baton, 18, 26
Bird's Nest Stadium, 21
Bolt, Usain, 4, 22
Bubka, Sergey, 30–31
Bulgaria, 33

C
cannonballs, 29
China, 21
Cuba, 32–33

D
decathlon, 7–15
denominator, 10
diagram, 24, 32, 36
discus, 5, 7, 14, 29, 36–37
division, 17, 21, 23, 26–27, 31

E
Eaton, Ashton, 12–13
El Guerruj, Hicham, 16–17
English, 9–16

F
fast walking, 7

G
Greece, 4–5, 21
Griffith-Joyner, Florence, 22–23

H
hammer, 7, 36
Hardee, Trey, 12
heptathlon, 7
high jump, 7, 24, 30–33
hurdles, 14, 19, 24–25

I
intersecting, 32
Isinbayeva, Yelena, 30–31

J
Jamaica, 4, 11, 22
javelin, 5, 7, 14, 28–29, 36–37
Johnson, Michael, 22–23

K
Koch, Marita, 22–23
Kostadinova, Stefka, 33

L
London Olympics (2012), 10
long-distance, 4, 7, 19
long jump, 5, 7, 14, 34

M
Masterkova, Svetlana, 9, 17
medals, 7, 9, 11, 23
meet, 39–45
meter, 14, 20, 23–26, 37
middle-distance, 7, 19–20
mile run, 9, 16–17, 20
Morocco, 16
Mount Olympus, 5, 21
multiplication, 24, 40, 42

N
Native American, 9

O
Olympic Games, 5–14, 18, 22–23, 27, 32–33

P
parallel, 32
pentathlon, 5, 7, 15
perpendicular, 32
Pistorius, Oscar, 22–23
pole vault, 7, 14, 30–31, 41

R
relay races, 7, 18–19, 23, 26–27, 39–44
rounding, 17, 23, 37
Rudolph, Wilma, 23, 26–27
Russia, 9, 11, 17, 30

S
scoring, 39–45
shot put, 7, 14, 29, 36–37, 41
Sotomayor, Javier, 32
South Africa, 22
sprinting, 7, 12, 19–27, 39, 41
subtraction, 12–13, 15–17, 20–21, 23, 25, 27, 30–31, 33, 35, 45
Sweden, 14

T
Thorpe, Jim, 9, 12–15
track stadium, 20–21, 27
triple jump, 7, 34–35, 39–45

U
Ukraine, 30, 33
United States, 11

W
Wieslander, Hugo, 14–15
wrestling, 5, 10

513 M   FIF
Murray, Stuart,
Score with track and field math /

FIFTH WARD
12/14